DEVOTIONS FOR THE SANDBOX SET

Devotions for the Sandbox Set

Jane Morton

ILLUSTRATED BY
SHARON DAHL

Chariot VICTOR
PUBLISHING
A DIVISION OF COOK COMMUNICATIONS

Chariot Books is an imprint of ChariotVictor Publishing,
a division of Cook Communications, Colorado Springs, Colorado 80918
Cook Communications, Paris, Ontario
Kingsway Communications, Eastbourne, England.

Text © 1997 by Jane Morton
Illustrations © 1997 by Sharon Dahl
Designed by Andrea Boven

First Printing, 1997
Printed in Canada
1 2 3 4 5 Printing/Year 01 00 99 98 97

ISBN: 1-56476-599-7

The following poems are reproduced by permission of their publishers:
"It's Me, God": Reprinted from "Pockets, June 1984. Copyright © 1984 by The Upper Room.
"Quiet Time": Reprinted from WOW, April 13, 1975. Copyright © 1975, American Baptist Churches in
the U.S.A., Board of Educational Ministries.
"A Question": Reprinted from Happy Times, September, 1975. Copyright © 1975 by Concordia
Publishing House.
"Cloud Pictures": Reprinted from WOW, July, 1974. Copyright © 1974, American Baptist Churches in
the U.S.A., Board of Educational Ministries.

Scripture taken from the Holy Bible: New International Version®. Copyright © 1973, 1978, 1984 by
International Bible Society. Used by permission of Zondervan Publishing House. All rights reserved.

To Liz,
who made this book possible.
J.M.

Thanks to Mom and Dad for making
my "sandbox" years so precious,
and to my sister for joining me
in that sandbox.
S.D.

CONTENTS

NOTE TO THE READER

Adult and child can sit down together to share this book.

Using the questions as a guide, take time to talk and think about God. Perhaps the Bible verses, the poems and the pictures will suggest other questions and lead to further discussion.

Feel free to follow the child's line of thinking wherever it goes.

May shared moments result in spiritual growth and leave participants with happy memories of time well spent.

Jane Morton

IT'S ME GOD

You've answered my prayers,
    So I know that You hear,
But so many voices
    Are reaching Your ear.
How can You know?
    Yet somehow You do—
It's me, God,
    It's me
Who is talking with You.

> *I call on you, O God, for you will answer me.*
> **PSALM 17:6**

Is God busy? What do you think He has to do? Do you ever have to wait to talk to Him? Is He there when you need Him? How do you know?

WHERE ARE YOU?

Sometimes I wonder where You are,
    And then I think of air.
I can't see or touch it, God,
    And yet I know it's there.

I feel Your love inside my heart,
    Your spirit everywhere.
I can't see or touch You, God,
    And yet I know You're there.

> *God is spirit, and His worshipers must worship in spirit and in truth.*
> **JOHN 4:24**

Where is God? How do you know? Have you seen Him? Have you felt Him near? When?

MY HOUSE

I have a house.
    It has a door.
It has a roof.
    It has a floor.
My house has walls
    And windows, too.
I live there, God,
    And so do You.

*I love the house
where you live,
O Lord.*
PSALM 26:8

*Where does God live? Does He live in your house? What makes you
think He does or He doesn't? Might He live in other people's houses? Does
He live outdoors? Does He live in the church?*

CITY STREETS

City streets
    Absorb the heat.
City sidewalks
    Burn bare feet.

Thank you, God,
    For rain that cools
And leaves behind
    Mud-puddle pools.

> *"I will send down showers in season; there will be showers of blessing."*
> **EZEKIEL 34:26**

How do your feet feel when you wade in a mud-puddle?
Who sends the rain? Why do we need rain?
How does God know what we need?

FORGIVE ME, GOD

I fought with my friend,
    And I came home mad,
For he was not willing
    To share what he had.

Now I think I was wrong.
    Please forgive me once more,
And I'll forgive him,
    As I go to his door.

> *"Forgive, and you will be forgiven."*
> **LUKE 6:37**

Is it easy to forgive people who have hurt you? Did you ever do things you wish you hadn't? Were you forgiven? Who forgave you?

ME FIRST

I'm not first,
    I'm number three.
You, then others,
    Then comes me.

> *Love the Lord your God with all your heart, and with all your soul, and with all your strength and with all your mind, and love your neighbor as yourself.*
> **LUKE 10:27**

Have you ever said, "me first"? Did you want to be first in line?
Have first turn? Be first to be served? Who should come first in our lives?
Who said this? Who should come second? Who taught us to put God first
and to love our neighbors as much as we love ourselves?

WHO IS MY NEIGHBOR?

My neighbors live next door to me,
  They live across the street.
They live in other parts of town
  Too far away to meet.

They live in other towns and states,
  They live across the sea.
They are the ones who need my help
  Wherever they might be.

Do you know your neighbors? What are their names?
Do you have neighbors you don't know? Where do they live?
How can you help neighbors you don't know or never see?

PRESCHOOL

First day of preschool
    I am new.
Other children
    May be too.

Help me make friends,
    And help me be
A friend to those
    Who may need me.

"I was a stranger and you invited me in."
MATTHEW 25:35

*Have you ever felt strange when you had to do something new?
Did anyone help you feel more comfortable? Have you ever made friends
with a new child? When have you ever invited a child who was a
newcomer to your home?*

WHEN I PRAY

When I pray
    I know You're near.
You are listening.
    You will hear.

> *Be merciful to me
> and hear my
> prayer.*
> **PSALM 4:1**

When do you pray? What are some of the things you pray for? Do you feel closer to God when you pray? How do you know He is listening?

MY FEARS

I fear all the things
    That come into my room,
The lion and tiger and bear.

But when I get up
    And look under my bed,
I find that they aren't even there.

When do you feel afraid? Are you scared of something real? What can you do about it? Do you believe God will take care of you?

SNOWFLAKES

Each snowflake is different.
   Each person is too.
How is it, I wonder,
   You do what You do?

In the poem, who is "You"? Have you ever looked at snowflakes under a magnifying glass? What did you see? Did all the snowflakes look alike? Are any two people exactly alike? Twins? Do you ever wonder how God makes everything so special?

ME

Eyes,
    Ears,
Mouth,
    Nose,
Arms,
    Hands,
Fingers,
    Toes,
Cheek,
    Chin,
Elbow,
    Knee.
Thank You, God
    For giving me
All the parts
    That make me, me.

For we are God's workmanship.
EPHESIANS 2:10

Touch your eye, ear, mouth, nose, your arm, hand, finger, toe, your cheek, chin, elbow, knee. As you touch each part of your body, think about how it works for you. How can you take care of the body God gave you?

WATER

Water in the ocean.
Water in the sink.
Water that I wash in.
Water that I drink.

Fish can't live without it.
People need it, too.
Thank You, God, for water.
Water comes from You.

How does water get into the sink? Where does our water come from? Could we get along without water? Why not?

BLOSSOM TIME

When blossoms, like popcorn,
  Cover the trees,
I hear the buzz, buzz, buzz
  Buzzing of bees.

Thank You for springtime
  And blossoms and bees,
And thank You for apples
  That come after these.

What season comes after spring? What season will it be when the apples are ready to eat? What season will come after that? Who sends the seasons?

CLOUD PICTURES

On hot and lazy summer days
    I watch the clouds drift by,
And I look up and try to find
    A picture in the sky.

I see a train, I see a bird,
    I see a polar bear.
I see a lamb, I see a ship
    Floating in the air.

The pictures come, the pictures go.
    They change each time I look.
That is why the summer sky
    Is God's own picture book.

> *There was the glory of the Lord appearing in the cloud.*
> **EXODUS 16:10**

Do you ever watch the clouds? What do you see? Who makes the clouds?

JESUS

Jesus healed the sick and the lame.
Jesus calmed the sea.
Jesus loved the children,
Little ones like me.

> *Let the little children come to me, and do not hinder them, for the kingdom of God belongs to such as these.*
> **MARK 10:14**

How do we learn about Jesus? What were some things He did while He was on earth? How do you know Jesus loved children?

HIDE AND SEEK

Hide and seek.
    Hide and seek.
I close my eyes.
    I do not peek.

Oly-oly-ox-in-free.
    Now I hide
Where friends can't see.

I can hide
    Where friends can't see,
But I can't hide
    From You or me.

> *"Can anyone hide in secret places so that I cannot see him?"* declares the Lord.
> **JEREMIAH 23:24**

Does God know where you are and what you are doing?
Where could you hide from God? Where could you hide from yourself?
Do you believe God knows everything?

A QUESTION

When clothes wear out,
    Where do they go?
Where is the cloth
    That covered my toe?

I have a hole
    Where the sock used to be,
And where the sock went
    Is what bothers me.

The sock is quite old,
    It's not that I care.
It's just that it's gone,
    And I'd like to know where.

> If any of you lacks wisdom, he should ask God.
> **JAMES 1:5**

Why does the sun come up every day? Where does it go when it sets? How do hummingbirds know to fly South in the fall? Why do swallows return in the spring? Does anyone know the answers to these questions? Does God know? Why does God know?

SUNDAY SCHOOL

I like to go to Sunday school.
   I learn about You there.
The teacher tells me of Your love.
   She tells me that You care.

Sometimes I hear a story
   Or learn a verse to say.
I like to go to Sunday school
   To worship and to pray.

> *I rejoiced with those who said to me, "Let us go to the house of the Lord."*
> **PSALM 122:1**

Do you go to Sunday school? What do you do there?
Can you think of something you learned?

AS I AM

I'm glad that You love me
   The way that I am.
I know I'm not perfect just yet.

I'll try to improve,
   And I hope that I do,
But You'll be there in case I forget.

> Be perfect...as your heavenly Father is perfect.
> MATTHEW 5:48

Is anybody perfect? Who? Does God love us even though we make mistakes? Should we try to be perfect (like Jesus), even though it's hard?

TEACH ME TO LISTEN

Teach me to listen
    When You speak to me,
Although I don't know
    When and where that might be.

You could speak with a voice
    That I hear in my ear,
Or a feeling inside me
    That tells me You're near.

You could come in a dream,
    And I'll know that You're there.
You could speak to me, Lord,
    Anytime, anywhere.

Help me be quiet
    And listen to You,
And do all the things
    That You want me to do.

How does God speak to us? Has He ever spoken to you?
What did He say?

QUIET TIME

I like to watch the stars come out,
    And see day turn to night.
Thank You for this quiet time
    and each small twinkling light.

The heavens declare the glory of God.
PSALM 19:1

Have you ever watched the stars come out? Tell what happened.
Did watching the stars come out make you think of God?
Can you count the stars? Why not?

BEDTIME

When I go to bed at night,
    I take my teddy bear.
I hold him close and hug him tight
    And tell him You are there.

> *Never will I leave you.*
> **HEBREWS 13:5**

Is God with you when you go to sleep? Will He leave you during the night? How do you know?

SHARING

A small boy shared
    His fish and bread
One day in Galilee,
    And Jesus fed the hungry crowd
Out there beside the sea.

Help me share as that boy did
    That day beside the sea.
Help me share with those in need
    The gifts You've given me.

How did one boy's lunch feed so many people?
Why should we share what we have?

THE DOOR

Jesus stands at the door,
 The door of my heart.
He's waiting outside to come in.

I'll open the door,
 The door of my heart,
And He'll fill me with love from within.

> Here I am!
> I stand at the
> door and knock.
> **REVELATION 3:20**

Why does Jesus want to come into your heart? How do we let Him come in?
Will you let Him come in?

MY BEST, BEST FRIEND

Jesus is my best, best friend.
    He loves and cares for me.
When I am sad and by myself,
    He keeps me company.

When I am sick, He's by my side,
    He never goes away.
Forever is a long, long time,
    But that's how long He'll stay.

*What is a friend? Do you have a best friend at school or in your
neighborhood? What is your friend's name? Did you ever have a friend
who moved away? How did you feel? Will Jesus ever move away?
How long will He stay? Can we ever make Him leave?*

LOVE

You give me Your love,
    And I give it away,
Yet it keeps coming back;
    I have more every day.
How does this happen?
    Oh, how can it be?
I'd like to have someone
    Explain it to me.

> *We love because He first loved us.*
> **1 JOHN 4:19**

*Where does love come from? Do you give your love to others?
Who are they? Do you give your love to God? How does the love
you give come back to you?*

ENERGY UP TO THE SUN

I'm going outside where I'll hop,
    skip and run.
For today I have energy up to the sun,
Energy up to the moon and the stars,
Energy up to the planet of Mars.
Thank You for life and for health
    and for fun.
Thank You for energy up to the sun.

"I have come that they may have life, and have it to the full."
JOHN 10:10

What is energy? Where does it come from? Why do we need it?
If you have energy up to the sun, how much energy do you have?
Who gives us life and health? What is joy?

FAMILIES

I'm drawing a picture
   Of Sister and me,
My mom and my dad
   By our big maple tree.
I'll draw our dog, Sport,
   And then I'll be done.
My family numbers
   Four people plus one.

Some families are big
   And some families are small.
All families are special,
   And You love them all.

Have we not all
one Father?
Did not one God
create us?
MALACHI 2:10

How big is your family? Do you have a pet? Is your pet part of your family? How is your family special? Did Jesus have a family? How was His family special? Who is our Father in heaven?

COLORS

The sky is blue,
    The grass is green,
And clouds of white
    Float in-between.

The yellow sun
    Shines down on me.
I thank You, God,
    For all I see.

What would the world be like if there weren't any sun?
What does darkness feel like? What are some other kinds of light?
What do we mean when we say, "Jesus is the light of the world"?

YOUR GIFT

You gave Your son,
    Your only son.
He came that we might live.
    You gave the world
The greatest gift
    That You could ever give.

> *For God so loved the world that He gave His one and only Son.*
> **JOHN 3:16**

What was the gift God gave us? Has God given us more than one gift? Can you think of other gifts from God?

TEN LEPERS

Jesus cured ten lepers,
    And nine went on their way.
One came back to thank Him
    For what He did that day.

Let me be quick to thank You,
    Just like that grateful one.
Thank You, God, for loving us,
    And thank You for Your son.

*What did it mean to be a leper? Why do you think nine of the lepers
didn't thank Jesus for healing them? Can you think of a time you might
not have thanked God for something He did for you? When?
Do you think God wants us to thank Him?*

BREAD

Thank You, God
     For bread we eat.
Thanks for farmers
     Growing wheat.
Thanks for bakers
     Baking loaves
In the ovens
     Of their stoves.
Thanks for sending
     Sun and rain.
Thanks for ripening
     The grain.
Without Your help
     There'd be no bread.
Thanks for helping
     Keep us fed.

Where does your bread come from? Did your family buy it at the store or did someone you know bake it? Where did the flour come from? Where did the grain that goes into the flour come from? How does God give us our daily bread?

MY STRENGTH

I am not big.
    I am not tall.
My muscles and
    My hands are small,
But with the strength
    That You give me,
I am as strong
    As strong can be.

> *The Lord is my strength and my song.*
> **EXODUS 15:2**

What kind of strength does God give us? Have you ever trusted that God would help you? When? Does God give a child strength too?

THROUGH HIM

Help me be like Jesus, God,
    In everything I do.
Through Him I learn to love and live.
    Through Him I come to You.

How can we learn about Jesus? How can we be like Him?
What did He teach us about love? What did He teach us about God?

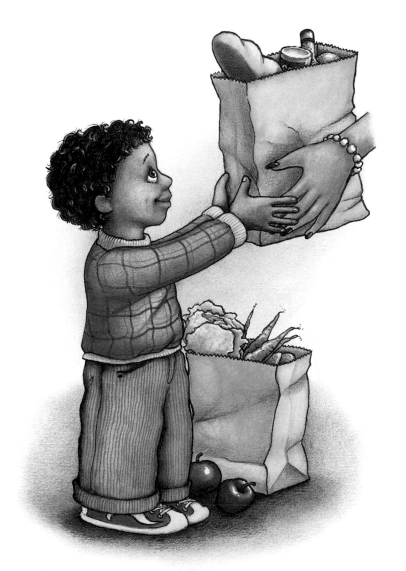

G-O-D

A B C D E F G
  Now I'm spelling
G-O-D.
  Just three letters
In Your name.
  G-O-D
Always the same.
  I love You,
And You love me.
  Just three letters,
G-O-D.

What do you think when you hear the word, "God"? Love? Father? Creator? What? Is God always there for you? Does He ever change? How do you know He always loves you?

MY GRIEF

My dog died, God, and I feel sad.
    And yet my eyes are dry.
He was the only dog I had.
    I hurt too much to cry.
I have an empty place inside,
    Because I miss him so.
Especially when I see his dish
    And places we would go.
I cannot even talk about
    How bad I really feel.
Put your arms around me, God,
    And help my heart to heal.

> *The eternal God is your refuge, and underneath are the everlasting arms.*
> **DEUTERONOMY 33:27**

Have you ever felt really sad? What made you feel this way?
Did you tell God about it? Did you share your feelings with anyone else?
Who? Did it help? How can God put His arms around us?
Did Jesus ever feel sad?

FOOTPRINTS

I walked along the beach one day
    Where water meets the land.
My sneaker soles left prints that looked
    Like waffles in the sand.

A wave came in and washed away
    The prints that followed me.
It moved the sand right over them,
    And they went out to sea.

When Jesus came to live on earth,
    He left His footprints here.
The prints He left lead us to God.
    They'll never disappear.

Have you ever left footprints in the sand or the mud?
How long did they last? Did Jesus leave footprints?
What kind of footprints did Jesus leave? Why haven't they disappeared?

THE MOON

Sometimes the moon
    Looks very small,
But really it's not
    Small at all.
Earth shadows
    Play a trick on me
By hiding part,
    So I can't see.

> *For we know in part.*
> **I CORINTHIANS 13:9**

Why might the moon change size? Should we believe everything our eyes tell us? Do you think we know everything there is to know about God? What are some things we don't know? Is it okay not to know or understand?

MY TRACK

Set an example
for the believers.
I TIMOTHY 4:12

When I leave
 A track in the snow,
Others may follow
 Wherever I go.
Through my behavior,
 I leave a track, too.
Others may follow
 Whatever I do.
Help me show others
 That You live in me,
And be the example
 You want me to be.

*Can you think of a time when you left tracks for others to follow?
Tell about it. Was there a time when you set a good example?
What did you do?*